Original title:
Tales from the Terrarium

Copyright © 2025 Creative Arts Management OÜ
All rights reserved.

Author: Zachary Prescott
ISBN HARDBACK: 978-1-80581-850-2
ISBN PAPERBACK: 978-1-80581-377-4
ISBN EBOOK: 978-1-80581-850-2

The Greenery Chronicles

In the corner of the room, a cactus wore a hat,
He danced alone, quite proud, said, "Look at that!"
The ferns all giggled, twirling in their pots,
While the geraniums rolled their eyes at the lot.

A potato voiced his dreams of seeing the sky,
"I want to be a French fry, oh me, oh my!"
The herbs chimed in, with a chorus of cheer,
"Let's hit the road, potatoes, we can steer!"

A gnome snored loudly, lost in a deep sleep,
While the snails played poker, bets in a heap.
"I fold!" said Lou, with a sly little grin,
"Let's get another round, let the games begin!"

The flowers threw a party, with pollen on the floor,
They tossed confetti made of leaves, and begged for more.

But the dog in the garden barked, looking quite perturbed,

"Hey, keep it down! This noise is absurd!"

Journeys in a Seed

In the bustle of dirt, a seed took a ride,
Rolling right past where the worms like to hide.
It shouted with glee as it bounced on a rock,
'I'm off to grow tall, just watch me unlock!'

With sunlight as fuel, it stretched out its leaves,
Dancing with laughter as it tangled in weeds.
The moon chuckled low, saying, 'What a sight!
A sprout with a dream, all ready for flight!'

Wonders of the Walled Garden

In a garden enclosed, the plants played a game,
'Who can grow fastest and earn all the fame?'
The carrots competed to add more sweet crunch,
While radishes giggled, all ready for lunch.

The roses turned royal, sporting their crowns,
While daisies wore frowns, just moping around.
'I wish I could bloom with such pizzazz too!'
'Just be yourself, sweet friend, that's the best view!'

Songs of the Substrate

In a world underground, the roots sang their song,
Beneath all the chaos, they'd twirl all day long.
'I'll tickle the soil, make the earth laugh,'
Said a bold little root named Ed, on his path.

They harmonized softly with a quirky tune,
'Let's tease the earthworms and dance to the moon!'
With each little wiggle, the soil shook with glee,
A concert of laughter, happy as can be!

Legends of the Living Layers

Once in a patch where the layers collide,
Lived a pot-bellied bug, with nowhere to hide.
He claimed he was king of the squishy old muck,
And challenged the critters, saying, 'I've got luck!'

The snail did a shuffle, the beetle wore shades,
As the fungi took bets on who'd win this charade.
With a wiggle and jiggle, and an oh-so-cool glide,
They spun tales of glory, oh what a wild ride!

The Dance of Dappled Light

In the sun's embrace, shadows prance,
Flickering whispers in a playful dance.
A lizard laughs, in shades of green,
While the beetles boogie, so keen and serene.

The petals spin in merry delight,
Catching the rays, oh what a sight!
Moths twirl and leap, bold in their quest,
While daytime critters take a rest.

The fungi giggle beneath the trees,
Tickled by thunders of passing breeze.
Sunbeams tumble in every nook,
Crafting a stage for the lively crook.

In this realm where light winks bright,
Even the shadows join the flight.
Every creature has its part to play,
In nature's folly, all sway and sway.

Saga of Serpentines

A wiggly wraith with a wink and a grin,
  Slithering fast, his journey begins.
The garden's alive with a squiggly cheer,
  As the snakes tell tales, drawing near.

Around the rocks, they twist and they twine,
  Riddling their paths, so serpentine.
With a flick of their tails, they do a jig,
  While frogs on logs applaud, oh so big!

One little snake thinks he's quite the star,
  Dreams of scales that can shine from afar.
He poses, he preens, in a patch of sun,
  But giggles erupt; he's so far from done!

A twist and a turn, then—whoosh! There he goes,
  Dodging a worm, oh how funny it flows!
In the heart of the greens, they weave and whine,
  In this merry garden, oh so serpentine.

Legends in the Leaf Lattice

Under the leaves, secrets unfurl,
Whispering legends in nature's whirl.
A snail with a crown, it's quite the sight,
Claims to be king from dawn until night.

The ladybugs gather for council in rows,
Deciding who reigns, well, nobody knows.
They giggle and glance at their friend on the ground,
While the ants march in, making a sound.

A squirrel chimes in with a tale of his own,
Of legendary acorns that dare to be sown.
With nutty ambitions, they scramble and scheme,
Chasing giggles in a humorous dream.

In this leafy realm, all's a big jest,
Even the wind seems to join in the fest.
With laughter as fuel for each plant and beetle,
The legends they weave are delightfully feeble.

Myriad Voices in Moss

In a green, soft kingdom where moss tends to sway,
Voices erupt in a playful bouquet.
A toad croaks hello, with a hop and a cheer,
While the crickets chirp, 'We're glad you are here!'

The mushrooms chime in with their quirky charm,
Offering laughter like a cozy warm farm.
With a splash of wet soil and scents sweetly rank,
The whole damp choir joins in, no one's too blank!

A centipede twirls, with a dance full of flair,
Every leg tapping with jest in the air.
With giggles abounding, the laughter takes flight,
As shadows and sunlight frolic so bright.

In this mossy wonder where fun never quits,
Every whisper, each chuckle, in nature it fits.
From the smallest of bugs to the grandest of trees,
In the mossy embrace, there's a giggle with ease.

The Secret Life of Succulents

In the sunlight, they strike a pose,
With their plump cheeks and little toes,
Underneath, they gossip and chat,
While plotting to take over the mat.

Cacti wear hats made of fluff,
While aloe thinks they're rather tough,
Dancing leaves in pots so round,
They share secrets, such joy is found.

With whispers of watering woes,
In their world, a tumbleweed goes,
They roll and laugh, what a sight,
Their party starts long past the night.

When the gardener walks on by,
They freeze and act like they're shy,
But once that door clicks to a close,
Their wild antics surely expose.

Parables of the Potted Paradise

In pots of clay, they weave their tales,
With vibrant hues and stubborn scales,
Basil flirts with a tomato vine,
As chives chuckle over good wine.

Each sprout has a dream to bloom,
With hopes of light in a dark room,
An oak leaf whispers to a fern,
"Chill out, buddy, it's your turn!"

Water droplets are fairy tears,
That cause the plants to face their fears,
They wiggle roots and wave their leaves,
In this garden, laughter never leaves.

Repotted and proud, they sing,
Delivering joy, now that's the thing,
From busy bees to sunlit skies,
Their stories paint the world in sighs.

Imprints of Insects

Tiny critters with grand designs,
Leave footprints on the leafy lines,
A ladybug dons its finest red,
While a centipede boasts of its spread.

Ants march in a parade so neat,
Bound for crumbs, their tasty treat,
The beetles play cards 'neath the shade,
As grasshoppers revel, unafraid.

With a twinkle, a fly buzzes by,
And the dragonflies chase in the sky,
Spiders weave tales in silken threads,
While praying mantises offer their heads.

On warm days, they stretch and show,
The funny dance of their bazaar flow,
Living life with a wink and a laugh,
In this garden of the quirky staff.

Serenade of the Shrubs

In the bushes where whispers loom,
A raucous group breaks into tune,
Hedgehogs hum and rabbits sway,
While flowers join in their ballet.

Burly bushes start a line,
"Let's show the daffodils they pine!"
With blooms that blush and petals bright,
They twirl together into the night.

Each leaf a note, each stem a beat,
Nature's band at yonder street,
They groove to the sun's sweet refrain,
As dusk falls softly through the lane.

When morning breaks, they rest their heads,
With antics tucked in cozy beds,
A funny serenade they play,
Beneath the sun, come what may.

Chronicles Hidden in Glass

Inside this glass domain, oh so bright,
The ants play poker each starry night.
Silly plants gossip, spreading their buzz,
While the goldfish dance, just because!

A worm thinks he's king, on a throne made of dirt,
He poses for worms, in his snazziest shirt.
The crickets sing loud, with a wink and a laugh,
As the snails start a race, but they take half a path!

The sunflowers smile, wear hats in great cheer,
The tomatoes plan parties, inviting all near.
In this wacky glass world, the fun never ends,
With mischievous critters and laughter from friends!

The Greenhouse Chronicles

In a world of tomatoes with dreams big and bold,
Cucumbers fashion a throne made of gold.
The radishes plot to become superheroes,
While the herbs throw confetti, and everyone knows!

The zucchini barista brews coffee with flair,
As the peppers debate, who's the fairest in there?
A strawberry slips on a leaf made of jade,
And the laugh that it lets out is truly a parade!

The toads in the corners sing songs of delight,
As the carrots tap dance, it's quite the sight.
In this greenhouse giggle, oh what a fun show,
With each quirky creature, the merriment grows!

Whispers in Glass

Behind the glass walls, the secrets unfold,
As the little green critters get feisty and bold.
The ladybugs chuckle, they're giggling so sweet,
While a wise old tortoise hums to the beat!

A curious fern tries to tell jokes so keen,
But the cactus just pricks it, if you know what I mean.
The butterflies flutter, painting the air,
With colors and giggles, a lively affair!

The snails hold a show with a slimy appeal,
With choreography perfect, a true garden reel.
In this glass-bound world, where whimsy is law,
The laughter of plants is the best thing you saw!

Secrets of the Soil

Beneath the rich soil, where secrets are kept,
The roots start a rumor, and giggling's inept.
The carrots wear shades, looking cool in their grime,
While the daisies do cartwheels, having a good time!

A chipmunk named Simon tells tales of the shroom,
As mushrooms chime in, making fun of the gloom.
The beetles recap every silly spree,
And the flowers can't stop, they just dance and agree!

The earthworms unite, forming clubs by the patch,
Debating the best way to bury a hatch.
In this hidden realm, beneath laughter and toil,
The secrets run deep, overflowing with soil!

Gleanings of Grasses

In the glade where grasses sway,
A frog in shades of green ballet.
He leaps and lands with such a cheer,
Announcing, "I'm the king right here!"

The crickets chirp a nightly tune,
While fireflies dance beneath the moon.
A squirrel, clad in nuts and pride,
Claims, "I'm the best! Just look, I glide!"

The grasshoppers sing their high-pitched song,
While ants march by, all day long.
With tiny coats and grand charades,
They plan their trips, just like parades!

So here in this green, laughter's felt,
Where every creature's dreams are dealt.
From twisty roots to leafy beams,
The world's a stage of funny schemes.

Flourishes in the Flora

Petals dressed in colors bright,
Daisies dance in pure delight.
A bee buzzes with gossip flair,
"Have you heard? The roses swear!"

In pots of whimsy, herbs take flight,
With basil boasting, "I'm outta sight!"
Thyme counters back, sharp as a tack,
"Oh please, you're merely a green snack!"

The ferns are flirting, oh so sly,
While sunflowers stretch to kiss the sky.
They gossip low, behind each leaf,
About the cactus, who's a bit… brief.

So stroll among this floral crowd,
Where flowers shout and plants are loud.
Each bloom a quirky, funny sight,
In a garden where joy takes flight.

Whimsy in the Wilderness

In the woods where shadows play,
A bear wears socks, what a display!
He trips and tumbles, makes a scene,
Declaring, "I'm a ballet queen!"

The raccoons in their masks so sly,
Plan heists for candy, oh my, oh my!
They giggle, scurry, dart like thieves,
While squirrels toss acorns like leaves.

A deer performs a stand-up show,
With jokes about the grass below.
Her friends all laugh, but pine trees sigh,
"For goodness' sake, just let it lie!"

So wander through this wacky land,
Where every creature lends a hand.
In nature's realm of giggles bright,
The whimsies bloom, a pure delight.

Spirits of the Succulent

In a pot where cacti grow,
A prickly party starts to glow.
With jokes so sharp, they laugh and tease,
While succulents sway in the warm breeze.

A jolly jade with a wink and grin,
Says, "I've got the best of skin!"
While aloe boasts of soothing ways,
"I'll cure your burns for all your days!"

The hen and chicks are having fun,
Playing tag beneath the sun.
With spiky hats and roots so deep,
They share their secrets, then take a leap!

So in this world of green delight,
Where laughter blooms both day and night.
Each succulent sings a little cheer,
In this pot of joy, we're all sincere!

Gossamer Tales of the Understory

In the shade where spiders spin,
A grasshopper hums, wearing a grin.
The mushrooms dance in a jittery row,
While worms in tweed coats steal the show.

A ladybug struts, a pompous sight,
While snails in bow ties glide through the night.
The ants hold a meeting, quite in the zone,
Debating if sugar is better than bone.

A frog in a crown croaks out a tune,
As fireflies twinkle, winking at the moon.
A caterpillar claims he's a butterfly new,
But everyone knows he just stuck like glue.

So here in the shadows between the leaves,
The critters conspire, making mischief with ease.
In a world so small, where laughter does swell,
The underworld giggles, who can tell?

Aureate Whispers of Illumination

In a jar where the glowworms glow,
A beetle tells tales of 'long time ago.'
With glittery wings, he twirls in delight,
While a cricket in glasses prepares for a fight.

The glow of the moons makes shadows parade,
A snail on a skateboard has nothing to trade.
The fireflies blink like stars in a trance,
As spiders deliver a stand-up romance.

Moths on a mission for sequins so bright,
Are drawn to the lanterns like moths in the night.
But the lights start to flicker, they scatter in haste,
Saying, "Next time, be quick, there's no time to waste!"

In a world filled with laughter, they swirl and play,
Under shimmering scenes, where the whimsy won't stray.
A light-hearted frolic in the humor-filled air,
In the golden glow, not a single soul cares.

The Untold Narratives of Green

In the lush, where the crickets compete,
A roach takes a bow, it's a sight so sweet.
With grass blades as swords, they clash with might,
While ladybugs giggle, taking flight.

A frog in a trench coat acts quite bizarre,
Claiming he's on his way to a car.
The toads raise their brows, unsure if it's true,
But they join in the laughter, as toads often do.

The chameleon changes to match the mood,
While a worm with a dream plans a leafy feud.
The vines start to tangle, the air fills with cheer,
As the stories unfold in worlds we hold dear.

In this green haven, beneath sunlit beams,
Life's a big joke and bursting with dreams.
The whispers of nature, they giggle and sing,
As the stories unfold with the joy they bring.

Shadows and Sunbeams in the Box

In the corners of boxes where shadows collide,
A lizard named Larry seeks refuge and pride.
He struts on a ledge, with swagger and flair,
While a snail on a scooter rolls by without care.

Beneath leafy canopies, secrets do creep,
As ants tell tall tales, their promise to keep.
They march in a line, each one with a hat,
Debating which cookie is best for a snack.

A gerbil with glasses surveys all around,
Says, "I'm the king, I wear the crown!"
While the worms in the dirt form a deep band,
Playing tunes in the soil, the best in the land.

As sunbeams peek through, laughter is found,
In this quirky little realm, life spins round and round.
With shadows as friends and fun to the max,
The box is alive with laughter and snacks.

Reflections of the Rainforest

In the jungle's embrace, a snail took a nap,
With a big leafy hat, it plotted its map.
A monkey swung by, with a mischievous holler,
"Don't fall asleep now! Or you'll miss the flower!"

A frog on a log tried to sing with delight,
But croaked out a tune that gave us a fright.
The toucan nearby laughed loud as can be,
Said, "That's not a song, it's a frog's comedy!"

Tales of Trellis and Time

On a trellis so old, a snail climbed with pride,
While a parrot exclaimed, "Take me on your ride!"
But the snail just replied, "Let me take my time,
For I'm winning this race with my pace and my rhyme!"

A squirrel dropped nuts, thinking they were gold,
But a hedgehog laughed, "They're just stories retold!
Gather them with care, you might find a friend,
In a world full of whimsy, there's joy to extend!"

The Lure of Leafy Labyrinths

In a maze of green leaves, a rabbit got lost,
He asked a wise turtle, "No matter the cost,
Can you help me escape this leafy delight?"
The turtle just chuckled, "Stay here for the night!"

A chameleon lounged, changing colors with ease,
He blended and joked, "I'm a breeze in the trees!"
With whispers of laughter, they danced through the vines,

In a joyful parade with the sun that shines!

Remnants of Roots

Beneath ancient roots, a critter had rolled,
Found treasures of past, stories nervously told.
A worm wiggled up, with a tale of its own,
"Life in the soil is where seeds are sown!"

A beetle described how it once flew so high,
But tangled in webs, learned to never rely.
With each twist and turn, they shared with great glee,
Remnants of laughter from roots in the tree!

In the Whispering Glass

In the jar, a tiny frog,
Wearing shades, a cool old cog.
He croaks a tune, a party vibe,
With glowworms doing their own jive.

A spider spins a disco ball,
While ants are having heaps of fun, y'all.
The grass grows legs and starts to dance,
While crickets hop, they seize their chance.

A snail was late, but rolls with flair,
Decked in sequins, he's quite the pair.
The beetles clap, they cheer so loud,
For every creature in the crowd.

At dawn, they sneak, no one can see,
The froggy DJ, just let it be.
When light arrives, the party ends,
They snooze till night—such crazy friends.

Secrets Beneath the Soil

Underground, a worm with sass,
Boasts of trips through blades of grass.
He tells of beans that stretch like dreams,
And whispers secrets in the seams.

A gopher wearing a top hat,
Showcases treasures, isn't that pat?
He guards his stash with all his might,
While roots hold meetings every night.

A mole performs their magic tricks,
Pulls out carrots, all slick and quick.
The mushrooms giggle, start to sway,
As moonlight joins the soil ballet.

Back up top, the garden smiles,
As critters gather, sharing styles.
What lies beneath, a hidden glee,
From underground, it's mini-spree.

Echoes of the Enclosed

In a glass dome, a parakeet sings,
Wearing tiny shoes, oh the bling!
His buddy, a lizard, shades so neat,
Dances alongside, tapping his feet.

A hamster rolls in a golden ball,
Chasing raindrops that start to fall.
They feast on snacks—cheese and sweets,
While a goldfish grooves to the beats.

With pebbles shaped like silly smiles,
They all parade in playful styles.
A sunbeam slips through glassy walls,
And cheers erupt; a laughing call.

At twilight, stories fill the air,
Each creature shares with love and care.
A spark of joy, a bond so true,
Within this glass, a world anew.

Chronicles of the Green Realm

In a leaf-boat, a snail sets sail,
With a tiny map that tells a tale.
His crew? A bug in a pirate hat,
Set for adventure—no time to chat!

They navigate through blades so tall,
Dodge rainstorms with their greenish brawl.
An army of ants, they march on cue,
With tiny drums, they beat it too.

Frogs gather round for the show,
With popcorn made of seeds and dough.
The flowers sway, with petals bright,
While lightning bugs dance in delight.

In the end, they toast to the night,
With dew drops sparkling, oh what a sight!
Each critter smiles, with hearts aglow,
In the green realm, together they grow.

Soliloquies of the Soil

The earth whispers secrets, oh so sly,
Worms hold court, wearing hats awry.
A bug with a monocle sips on dew,
While roots giggle softly at the morning hue.

Poking fun at each passing ant,
'This tiny grand show? We hear every chant!'
Dirt prattles on, with a gregarious cheer,
In this patch of green, laughter is near.

A pebble chuckles at the ant's parade,
'Your work's a fine jest, but I'm not afraid!'
The daisies laugh, their heads held high,
'Bending with giggles, we'll reach for the sky.'

The soil concludes with a hearty guffaw,
'In the grand garden jest, there's always more to draw.'
With every tickle of rain on their cheek,
The earth chortles out, 'Life's never bleak!'

Vibrations of the Verdant

In the leafy realms where laughter sways,
Frogs in tuxedos plan grand displays.
A caterpillar winks, in a sequined thread,
'You call that a leap? Here, let's play instead!'

The ferns shimmy, waving their fronds,
While a wise old owl recites whimsical bonds.
A bee in a bowtie buzzes by,
Mocking a butterfly's flamboyant sigh.

'Pollen for snacks? How very quaint!'
Laughs the loud cricket, a musical saint.
Together they dance in the sun's golden rays,
Vibrations of joy fill the verdant maze.

As stars twinkle down in the evening light,
The laughter continues, a charming delight.
In this happy patch, where all creatures converse,
Life's a grand jest, and nature's the verse.

Diaries of Detritus

In the compost corner, treasures abound,
Where banana peels and old leaves confound.
A slug writes a diary of long, slimy days,
Documenting all in comical ways.

'Today's sunshine was really quite rare,'
Scribbles a snail, with meticulous care.
He recounts his slow stroll to visit a cat,
Who offered him pizza, though he's allergic to fat.

A garlic clove chuckles, recalling past fights,
With onions and leeks under twinkling lights.
'It's funny how we all tend to blend,
In this quirky world where all flavors mend.'

The compost heap chuckles, a grand buffet,
Everyone's welcome, no need for dismay.
In the diaries penned by the scattered debris,
Life's wittiest tales are as rich as can be!

Secrets of the Serpent

A snake in the grass whispers with glee,
'Now hear me unravel this twisted decree!'
With scales glimmering under the sun's golden light,
He rumbles along, ready for a delight.

'Today I slithered past the funny old frog,
Who mistook me for lunch, what a silly slog!'
He coils in laughter at the thought of the chase,
'The joke's on him, I have stealth and grace.'

A nested lizard leans, snickering sly,
'Your pranks are quite wicked, oh my oh my!'
With each flip of the tail, secrets are spun,
In the snake's secret world, oh, what fun!

As shadows stretch long and the sun starts to dip,
Our serpent concludes with a cheeky quip.
The funniest tales from the forest come alive,
In the whispers of scales, the best jokes survive!

Fragmented Lives in Crystalline Forms

In a jar full of glee, there's a snail on a spree,
He dances on leaves, sips the dew like it's tea.
A lizard's on break, playing tag with the light,
While whispers of moss giggle soft in the night.

A fly wears a crown made from glittering dust,
His subjects—a chorus of grubs that are just.
The ants hold a rally, oh what a fine show,
Debating if sugar or salt is the go!

In corners of glass, a frog plays the part,
Of a prince, with a leap that could steal any heart.
With a jump and a splash, he declares with a grin,
"Life's better in terrariums, let the fun begin!"

So raise up your glass, let's toast to the small,
In worlds of their own, they throw the grandest ball.
With a wink and a nod, they keep us amused,
These fragmented lives, wonderfully fused.

The Vibrant Fugue of Nature

In the heart of the glass, a party's begun,
Where the critters all gather, just basking in fun.
A parrot named Pete sings a tune so absurd,
That even the goldfish stop swimming, they've heard!

The plants sway in rhythm, with roots that can dance,
While a cricket on strings gives the beetles a chance.
They're jiving and jiggling with such giddy zest,
In this lively affair, nature's felt at its best.

But wait, what's that noise? It's a ruckus indeed,
The hedgehog in stripes has mistaken a seed!
"For dinner or for dessert, I can't seem to tell,
But either way, boy, this feast will be swell!"

So let's raise our salad, let's cheer for the crew,
In the twists of this world, every moment's brand new.
With laughter and munching, we'll fill up our hearts,
In this vibrant fugue, where each melody starts.

Stories of the Surface and Depth

On the surface, they laugh, with bubbles of cheer,
A raccoon's gone fishing with the fish he holds dear.
There's chatter and splashes, a festival bright,
As the water beetle's polishing up for the night.

Beneath in the shadows, the secrets do creep,
With the shy little worms who just want their beauty sleep.
They all jive together, the deep and the high,
Sharing tales of the sun and the midnight sky.

A turtle in shades recounts sights he has seen,
While a dragonfly dreams of being a queen.
"But darling," she muses, "I am far too small,
To rule over chaos, so I'll just have a ball!"

So stick to your stories, both bold and discreet,
In this wondrous ensemble, life is a treat.
From the surface to depth, with chuckles and grins,
Each moment's a treasure, where the laughter begins.

The Boughs of Imagination

In a world made of twigs and a roof of bright leaves,
A squirrel named Sam wears a hat that deceives.
He's the mayor of dreams in a kingdom of fluff,
Where acorns are treasures and magic's enough.

The branches are bustling with chatter and cheer,
As the owls spin tales no one wants to hear.
"When the sun starts to set and the fireflies play,
We party all night in the weirdest of ways!"

From the tips of the boughs to the roots deep below,
The critters unite in a festival flow.
With laughter as loud as the raccoon's dumb joke,
And a chorus of chirps where the night hums and spoke.

So come join the fun, let your thoughts take their flight,
In this playground of wonder, everything feels right.
Under boughs of imagination, they spring and they twirl,
In a whirling delight of a tiny, wild world.

The Adventures of Tiny Beings

In a world so small, with critters galore,
A beetle danced on a lily, wanting more.
The ants had a party, the crickets sang loud,
While a snail stole the limelight, feeling quite proud.

A butterfly teased, fluttering by,
The grasshoppers chuckled, on whispers they fly.
With mushrooms as tables, they feasted with glee,
Who knew tiny lives could be so carefree!

A curious worm wiggled out for a peek,
The ladybugs giggled, 'Are you lost, little sneak?'
Through tunnels they burrowed, a maze made of fun,
In their miniature world, the laughter outran the sun.

Beneath moonlit shadows, they danced 'till the dawn,
With twinkling star wishes, their worries were gone.
In a realm so bizarre, where all could belong,
These tiny beings knew that life's just a song.

Fables of Fern and Flora

The ferns told a story of a mischievous cat,
It knocked over a pot and then sat on the mat.
With a flick of its tail and a curious meow,
It became king of plants, taking a bow.

A cactus chimed in, pricking up its fate,
"Dear fern, do you mind if I stay out late?"
With a poke and a joke, they laughed for a while,
Their friendship was spiky but always worthwhile.

A daisy in bloom decided to spin,
Telling tales of the squirrels, where should they begin?
Nut stashes and forest races, oh what a ball,
These fables of flora could amuse one and all.

As the evening approached, they giggled and played,
While the fireflies gathered, a shimmering parade.
In a pot full of laughter, the night felt so bright,
These fables of ferns turned darkness to light.

Stories in a Glass Haven

Within a glass dome, world tiny and neat,
A lizard displayed its magnificent feat.
It somersaulted over a pebble with flair,
An audience of moss gave a shocked little stare.

The fish took a swim, sparkling like gold,
While a gnome told some jokes, delightfully bold.
The plants whispered secrets of sun and of rain,
In stories of growth, they'd giggle, not feign.

One day a brave ant, with a hat made of leaves,
Gave a speech to the crowd, 'I hope no one grieves!
Life's too short for worries, let laughter be free,
Now who wants to join me for a dance by the bee?'

As the moments unfolded, the fun never ceased,
All creatures were smiling, enjoying the feast.
In this glassy arena, life sparkled anew,
Where stories in harmony formed laughter's debut.

Whispers of the Wild Within

In the heart of a garden, where the wild things play,
A rabbit wore glasses, declared, 'Hip-hip-hooray!'
It taught the wise owls how to read between lines,
And squirrels brought snacks, cracking jokes 'neath the pines.

A hedgehog in sneakers ran races with glee,
While moths played the drums on an old wooden tree.
In whispers of laughter, the plants had a say,
They jived with the wind, tapping roots in ballet.

The wildflowers burst into giggles and spins,
As the bees formed a band for a grand jazzy din.
A toad added bass with a croak and a cheer,
Painting whispers of joy, turning woes into cheer.

So if you hear laughter, know it's no sin,
For it's wild things convening, it's fun to begin.
In nature's own kingdom, where stories unwind,
The whispers of wild give a joy to mankind.

Portents of the Petal Path

A snail wore a hat, oh what a sight,
His friends laughed so hard, they took flight.
A ladybug danced on a juicy red rose,
In a disco of petals, they struck playful poses.

A beetle recited, with much flair,
While a worm asked, "Is that a musical chair?"
The flowers all giggled, swayed side to side,
In their garden of laughter, they took much pride.

The mint leaves whispered secrets galore,
Of cats that would chase but couldn't keep score.
A butterfly joined, spreading good cheer,
With jokes about nectar that tickled the ear.

So shoo away worries, take a stroll near,
In the land of the giggles, where all is clear.
Where petals lead pathways to comical scenes,
And laughter blooms bright in the grass, oh so green.

Lingering in the Lush

In the grass sat a frog with a crown on his head,
He croaked out a tune while munching on bread.
Next to him, a squirrel flipped a nut with a spin,
Declaring, "In my show, I always win!"

A rabbit jogged by, in its fanciest shoes,
"Who knew I could hop?!" he exclaimed with the blues.
A butterfly winked, fluttering close,
"I've seen better dancers, just so you know!"

The ferns waved their fronds, laughing all the while,
"Join us for tea, we'll chat and compile!"
So together they stayed, under the sun's flush,
In a laughter-filled garden, happily lush.

With stories and giggles, and the tiniest snacks,
They left all their troubles to relax at the tracks.
No moss will grow here, just joy and mirth,
In this haven of laughter, the silliest berth.

Songs of Subterranean Spirits

Deep in the soil, where the gnomes like to play,
They strum on roots, making music all day.
With shovels for drums, they keep up the beat,
While earthworms do the cha-cha, oh what a feat!

The rocks chimed in, creating a sound,
Like maracas shaking where magic is found.
Together they sang of the daffodil's dance,
And how in the darkness, even seeds take a chance.

A mole wore a tie, looking quite grand,
He waved to the beetles, a formal demand.
"Come join the fiesta, let's dig through the night,
With tunes made of soil, it'll be such a sight!"

So listen, dear friend, when you wander around,
For laughter and music are buried in ground.
Just sit very still, let the giggles arise,
From the songs of the spirits, beneath deep blue skies.

Idyls of the Ideal Green

In a patch of pure grass, a cat took a nap,
While dreaming of fish and a big, comfy lap.
A butterfly landed, whispered, "Naptime is bold!"
Then tickled the cat, to a tale to be told.

A wise old toad croaked, "You look quite absurd,
To dream about fish when there's fun to be heard!"
And off they all scampered, to chase after light,
In the sprightly green world, 'neath the moon's twinkling bright.

The daisies had jokes that made everyone roar,
While moss shared its wisdom, both ancient and more.
The humor was rich, like the soil so deep,
Where giggles would echo and excitement would leap.

So gather your friends, take a stroll through the vale,
In the ideal green realms where laughter won't fail.
For in fields full of joy, each moment's a scene,
Of whimsical wonder, where life's always keen.

Enigmas of the Ecosystem

In the jungle, a sloth took a dare,
He tried to race with a flying hare.
But pacing slow under branches wide,
He lost the race and just sighed with pride.

A bird with a hat sang tunes quite absurd,
It rapped to the worms, who couldn't be stirred.
They wiggled and squirmed, quite lost in the beat,
Dancing in dirt, they shuffled their feet.

A frog made a wish on a sun-kissed rock,
To turn into prince as he watched the clock.
But when he leaped high, what a splash he found,
He landed in mud, and laughed all around.

A wise old snail with a shell polished bright,
Told tales of the stars on a cool, starry night.
But when asked for proof, he just shrugged and said,
'You'd have to be slow to see where they tread.'

Parables of the Plants

A cactus complained of its prickly attire,
'Everyone runs, I just quench their fire!'
But one day a bee wore a crown made of thorns,
It buzzed through the garden, adorned like a king's scorn.

The daisies decided to hold a grand ball,
Rainbow petals swirling, they invited them all.
But the tulips stood proud, in their vases of glass,
'We won't join your fun; just look at our class!'

A vine climbed so high it embraced the sun,
But tangled its roots, and now it can't run.
'The sun's my best friend,' it proudly would shout,
Yet its neighbor the fern just laughed and turned out.

The oak told a joke about squirrels and rain,
It chuckled so hard it shook off a pain.
But the acorn beneath said, 'I don't see the fun,'
'I'm just waiting to grow, and get out of the pun!'

Reveries of the Rewind

A turtle once dreamed he could break the sound,
He'd zoom through the field, and leap off the ground.
But each time he tried, just fell with a thud,
And laughed at the idea of soaring through mud.

The rabbit recalled how he lost to a snail,
In a race full of twists, he was doomed to fail.
He trained every day but lost with a grin,
Now he bets on the tortoise, who just lets him win.

A goldfish who wanted to jump out and fly,
Fell back with a splash, while letting out a sigh.
'I thought I could soar, it was quite a charade!'
Turns out swimming's better, less chance of a raid.

A hedgehog once pondered the stars in the sky,
'What do they whisper, and how do they fly?'
Yet after a while, he fell fast asleep,
With dreams of bright comets, those secrets to keep.

The Echoes of Ecospheres

In a pond where the frogs had a karaoke night,
They croaked out their songs, much to their delight.
But a fish in the deep thought it lacked some flair,
So he flipped on the stage, said, 'Let's really share!'

A parrot with thoughts of being a star,
Painted its feathers, though just from afar.
When it finally swooped in to claim all the cheers,
It landed so hard that it burst into tears.

A squirrel once entered a dance-off in shade,
With moves that amazed, it had it all made.
But a wise owl hooted, 'You dance like a fool,
Try rhythm instead, and you'll rule this cool pool.'

And so in the woods, where all creatures prance,
Laughter and joy follow each silly chance.
With mischief and glee, they embrace the bizarre,
No echo is lost, for we're all stars by far!

The Enchanted Biosphere

In a jar where the plants wear hats,
Tiny creatures dance like acrobats.
A snail with shades glides on a leaf,
While the ants plot a heist, oh what a thief!

A frog telling jokes, oh what a sight,
Dancing to the tunes of the moonlight.
The cacti giggle at a pun so dry,
While a beetle hums a lullaby.

A toad with a pipe, he's quite the bard,
Reciting tales, but they're all quite marred.
The soil winks every time it rains,
And the vines have secrets that spark like chains!

In this glass world, laughter's the creed,
Each critter and plant all join in the lead.
So if ever you peek, do come and stay,
Life in here is always at play!

Mythos of the Microcosm

In a speck of dirt, a saga unfolds,
Giant ants sailing on breadcrumbs like gold.
A caterpillar queen, full of demand,
Rules her domain with a soft, squishy hand.

The dust mites gather, it's party time,
With cakes made of crumbs and heaps of grime.
They're boogying down to the moldy beat,
Wiggly and giggly — oh, what a feat!

A roach in a tux, he leads the dance,
While the ladybugs giggle, given a chance.
The pill bugs roll by in a funny parade,
All claiming it's fun in this little glade.

Though the world seems small, the fun's quite grand,
With mischief galore in this tiny land.
So come take a peek, don't be shy,
For the humor thrives where the critters lie!

Vignettes from the Verdant Vault

In a leafy nook where the shadows play,
Squirrels perform acrobatics in a ballet.
A tree stump giggles, it's quite a hoot,
While mushrooms debate in their little suit.

The grass blades gossip as the wind does blow,
While worms share stories, all lined up in a row.
A ladybug jokes, saying, "I'm a star!"
She fixes her spots, "Have you seen my car?"

The frogs all agree, "Tonight's the night!"
With fireflies blinking, they spread the light.
A party erupts in this green little space,
With critters and plants all keeping pace.

So if you wander and find this scene,
Join in the laughter, keep the spirit keen.
For these vignettes, oh, they surely amuse,
In the vault where the verdant life brews!

Narratives of the Nurtured

Under a dome, where the wild things grow,
Chinchillas telling tales with a humorous flow.
A turtle in a top hat, oh what a sight,
Claims he runs faster — it's all in his might!

The ferns whisper secrets to the tall trees,
As crickets perform their night symphonies.
A slim beetle's got moves as he spins around,
While the spiders chuckle without making a sound.

In the corners, mischief brews with great glee,
As the goldfish plot their next big spree.
With bubbles of laughter floating in air,
Life's never dull in this vivacious lair.

So heed my advice, if you ever stop by,
Bring your own jokes, don't be shy, don't be shy!
For the narratives flourish in full, vibrant bloom,
In the cozy confines where all is in bloom!

Etchings in Evergreens

In the woods where squirrels dance,
They wear tiny hats at every chance,
With acorns stacked in silly piles,
They giggle in their nutty styles.

A rabbit paints with berry juice,
In colors bright, he's quite the recluse,
But when the owl comes to stare,
He dashes off, without a care.

The deer try tapping feet in time,
To beats that sound all out of rhyme,
With twirls and spins, they claim the floor,
And leave the trees to ask for more.

A raccoon juggles shiny things,
Each drop a laugh while laughter rings,
He's caught in moonlight's funny glow,
A master show, as night winds blow.

Fables in Ferns

Once a frog on a lily pad,
Told the world it wasn't bad,
With every croak, he sang a tune,
And made the flowers sway in June.

A turtle slow with tales to spin,
Said he could still outpace the wind,
With every step that took a while,
He wore a truly goofy smile.

A ladybug lost her pointy hat,
She searched for it beneath a mat,
With lady friends, they danced in circles,
While dodging raindrops that were merciless.

At twilight, shadows start to dance,
The critters join in merry prance,
Each whisper shared brings giggles grand,
In every nook of this green land.

The Hidden Harmony

In the garden, ants march proud,
Silent workers in their crowd,
With tiny hats made of tree bark,
They cluck and clammer till it's dark.

A butterfly sings off-key notes,
As the bees buzz in mismatched coats,
They gather round for evening cheer,
With their banter, laughter's near.

Oh, the hedgehog tries to rhyme,
But his prickly quills make it a climb,
His poems all roll like tumbleweed,
Yet filled with heart, it's what we need.

Night critters join this wacky show,
With moonlit beams, they steal the glow,
In laughter shared through every sound,
A symphony in fun is found.

Reflections of Resilience

A snail pondered his humble race,
Slime trails traced like a funny lace,
With every inch, he'd shout with glee,
"Life's a marathon, come run with me!"

A chameleon tried to blend in fast,
Changing colors, making laughs last,
But every time he switched too quick,
He'd turn bright pink, then a shade of sick.

The goldfish bubbled tales in the bowl,
Of pirate treasures and gallant souls,
With every splash, the tales would grow,
In watery worlds, their silly show.

Through ups and downs, a real delight,
They'd find the fun in every plight,
With smiles wide and hearts that sing,
In every nibble, joy's the thing.

Echoes of Enclosed Eden

In glassy halls where critters play,
A frog's big leap leads the way.
A snail on a mission, oh what a sight,
Takes hours to cross, it's quite the plight.

The turtle tells jokes that make us sneeze,
While crickets chirp, just doing as they please.
A dance of shadows, a lizard's twist,
In this little world, nothing is missed.

Tiny plants form a green brigade,
A cactus grins, yet shows no blade.
In this Eden, all is delight,
Even the dust bunnies take to flight.

So here we laugh in our glassy dome,
Where every bug feels right at home.
Each day's an adventure, wild and free,
In this tiny jungle, just you and me.

Chronicles of the Canopy

Up high in the foliage, tales unfold,
A squirrel's quest for nuts, so bold.
It stashes acorns, forgets the score,
Then wonders why he can't find more!

Beetles hold court on a leaf's grand chair,
Debating the best way to get somewhere.
With wings so fancy, they take to air,
But end up tangled, what a silly affair!

The mischievous monkey drops a vine,
Spots a grasshopper, oh how divine!
A leap and a hop, but down he goes,
And land on a cactus, who'd have supposed?

In the canopy's chaos, laughter rings,
Each creature a jester in nature's flings.
So come join the fun, leave worries below,
In this leafy realm, let silliness flow.

Stories Beneath the Moss

Under soft green blankets, critters convene,
A slug plans a feat, a shiny machine.
With wheels made of leaves, and glue from the earth,
It zooms through the grass, a wild rebirth!

Ants hold a race in a glistening trail,
Each one designed with a grand tale.
The winner's a cheater with stickers of gold,
But nobody sees him, or so he's told!

A wise old worm tells puns with flair,
While mossy cushions become their chair.
Giggles erupt at each clever quip,
In this underground cabaret, it's quite the trip!

So dive beneath shadows where the giggles start,
In nature's soft theater, partake, take part.
With laughter as fuel, adventure in store,
In the heart of the moss, we'll always want more.

Dreams in a Jar

In a bottle of dreams where the crickets sing,
A tiny garden hosts everything.
Jellybean flowers bloom with a smile,
While honeydew dew sits for a while.

A mouse on a trike zooms round and 'round,
While sunbeams dance on the colorful ground.
The fireflies twinkle, a disco delight,
As nighttime wraps up this charming sight.

Bottled laughter bubbles, a fizzy tease,
With gummy worms doing the cha-cha with ease.
In this whimsical jar, dreams twist and twirl,
A world full of giggles, a fantastical whirl!

So cheers to the quirky, the madcap, the light,
In this glassy domain, everything's bright.
Join in the fun, let your worries all part,
In a jar full of dreams, find the joy in your heart!

Rhythms of the Reptile

The lizard danced with such great flair,
His wiggly wiggle caught the air.
Frogs croaked beats, the turtles cheered,
In this wild show, no one appeared.

A snake slid by with a funky groove,
While geckos swayed, they found their move.
With every splash and silly hop,
The reptile party just won't stop!

A chameleon tried to steal the scene,
Changing colors, oh so keen!
But fell in a puddle of mud and muck,
Now he's a blunder, oh what luck!

So join the fun, do not delay,
Where scales and tails will laugh and play.
In this world of wiggles and wobbles galore,
The rhythm of reptiles will leave you wanting more!

Voices of the Verdure

In the garden, whispers rise,
Plants gossip under sunny skies.
The daisies giggle, tulips shout,
While tiny ants run round about.

The oak tree hums a sleepy song,
While ferns sway gently all day long.
Cacti crack jokes, they cactus jive,
In this green realm, all come alive!

The ivy's a rascal, climbing high,
Singing out loud as the butterflies fly.
"Hey leaf, be careful!" the petunia calls,
"Don't tumble down from those leafy walls!"

With roots entwined and laughter shared,
In this verdant space, all are prepared.
Nature's comedy is quite the show,
In the voices of the verdure, giggles flow!

Portals of the Plant World

Through a cactus door, adventure waits,
Leaves open wide, they tempt the fates.
What lies beyond in this green expanse?
A broccoli ball; come join the dance!

Vines twist and twirl like acrobats,
While sunflowers wear their sunny hats.
In this garden of glee, who wouldn't roam,
With every bloom, you feel at home?

A dandelion sneezes, oh what a sight!
Sending puffs of fluff into the night.
Roses start giggling, their thorns held tight,
As petals release that sweet fragrance light.

Adventure awaits through each leafy gate,
In this plant world's giggle, we celebrate.
Where roots dig deep and joy's unfurled,
Explore the wonders of the plant world!

Homilies of Humus

In the dark of soil, wise words abound,
Worms share secrets beneath the ground.
"Don't rush like the wind," the compost croaks,
"Life's best lessons come with some yolks!"

Rich humus guffaws, "I'm quite the treat,
Mix a bit of dirt, and it's hard to beat!"
Grasshoppers nod, and daisies beam,
In this underground, a happy dream.

"Sharing's the key," says a wise old root,
"Just sprinkle kindness like a sweet fruit."
And when you dig deep, you'll always find,
Gems of laughter that leave you aligned.

So listen close to humus' tales,
The soil's true wisdom never fails.
In laughter and love, let the garden bloom,
With homilies of humus, there's always room!

The Enchanted Ecosystem

In a jar where critters dance,
The beetles boast of their great chance.
Mice declare their tiny rule,
As ants parade, a comical school.

Sparkling dust, a fairy's blight,
A snail claims it's sheer delight.
The grasshoppers laugh, hopping along,
While the worms hum a silly song.

Springtails skitter, like tiny jets,
Making bets on who forgets.
The smell of veggies fills the air,
As the hedgehogs split the fair!

Every leaf has a tale or two,
With gnomes that giggle, just for you.
Invisible mushrooms hold a feast,
Oh what fun, never ceased!

Chronicles of the Canopy

Up above in leafy sprawl,
A squirrel juggles acorns, a little ball.
Frogs leap about on a sticky pad,
While butterflies flirt, it's quite the fad.

The sun drops down in a silly way,
Chasing shadows that laugh and play.
A raccoon tips over his midnight snack,
As fireflies dance, they won't hold back.

Owl hoots, it's a wobbly tune,
While the crickets chirp, giving their boon.
The whole forest whispers, full of cheer,
In this crown of greens, there is no fear.

With every rustle, secrets spill,
Laughter lingers, never still.
Join the feast, it's a merry plight,
In the canopy's embrace, all is right.

The Hidden World Assembled

Beneath the stones and twigs so sleek,
A brigade of critters peek and squeak.
A mole digs deep, making quite a show,
While the ladybugs giggle, watching below.

The beetles march in lines, so proud,
Whispering secrets to a curious crowd.
A shy hedgehog rolls in a little ball,
While pinky worms wiggle, never small.

Fluttering sprites with wings of glee,
They steal the mushrooms, raising a spree.
The whole world's a party, don't you see?
As laughter erupts, it's pure folly!

Gather round for a whimsical show,
Where laughter and mischief freely flow.
In the hidden depths, tales unfold,
A world assembled, bright and bold.

Symphony of Life's Microcosm

Tiny violins play in the grass,
While crickets join in, full of sass.
A caterpillar's dream of wings to fly,
Making a scene, oh me, oh my!

The ants spin tales of feats so grand,
As spiders weave webs, at their command.
A chorus of wonders, buzzing with cheer,
In this little world, there's nothing to fear.

Beetles clap in rhythmic lines,
While the mushrooms sip on fragrant wines.
Even the rocks join in the fun,
Cheering along as day is done.

So let's take a bow to this charming show,
Where even the smallest can steal the glow.
In this microcosm, life takes flight,
A symphony of joy, pure delight.

The Secret Garden of Stories

In a pot of tales, the herbs conspire,
Whispers of mint take flight like fire.
Basil tells jokes that tickle the sun,
While thyme spins yarns that are second to none.

A cactus with spines sits smug and proud,
Snickers at daisies, all fluffy and loud.
The violets blush when the sun comes around,
A garden of laughter where joy can be found.

The lettuce is gossiping, crisp and so bright,
Sharing the secrets of the moonlit night.
Squashes plot mischief, the peas just can't wait,
For orbs of sweet stories on their big plate.

With each little sprout, another joke blooms,
In this patch of wonders, the fun never looms.
Giggles from roots twirl up to the sky,
In this secret garden, we all laugh and sigh.

Rooted Reveries

Beneath the soil, the whispers grow,
Worms wear their glasses like a funny show.
A carrot dreams big, with visions so grand,
While radishes snicker and clap their green hands.

The gnarled old oak offers wise-crack replies,
To tales of the daisies and their playful lies.
A gopher debates the worms in a race,
With a crown made of dandelions on his face.

The ferns share secrets of who danced with dew,
While roots strike a pose, as roots often do.
Each dream from the soil, a giggling delight,
Where laughter and growth hold hands in the night.

These rooted reveries twist and twirl,
As nature's own jesters unfurl and unfurl.
In the depths of the earth, a comedy blooms,
With punchlines and quips that light up the rooms.

Flights of Fancy in the Flora

Once a ladybug flew to see the blooms,
He promised the roses he'd bring all the tunes.
While daisies waltzed and hibiscus swayed,
The lilacs chimed in, bright colors displayed.

Bees formed a band, buzzing sweet melodies,
While butterflies twirled in the gentle, warm breeze.
Ferns did the conga, all leaves in a line,
As petunias giggled, "Hey, this is divine!"

In the shade of the oak, the laughter did blend,
With jokes whispered softly, the fun had no end.
A sunflower juggled raindrops and light,
While all of the petals joined in on the night.

The cosmos chuckled as stars lit the scene,
In this floral fiesta, all creatures convene.
Each flight of fancy took wing with delight,
In a garden of whimsies, all merry and bright.

Captured Dreams in Glass

In jars of green, dreams wiggled with cheer,
While a snail on a leaf said, "Don't forget me here!"
The moss told a story, bright emerald shine,
Of past playful nights in the curled silver vine.

A ladybug dined on a feast made of light,
Sipping on nectar, oh what a sweet sight!
The dragonflies danced, their wings all aglow,
In the watery glass where the fireflies flow.

The pebbles giggled, their hues bright and clear,
Telling tall tales that only they hear.
Gravel grinned widely, as twigs played their part,
In this snug little realm holding dreams close to heart.

Captured in glass, where the magic can stay,
The flora and fauna all frolic and play.
With laughter and joy, they sparkle like dew,
In this whimsical world where dreams feel so true.

Unfolding the Untamed

In a pot with a frog, what a sight,
He croaks tales of bugs, oh so bright.
His neighbor, a snail, takes it slow,
Dreaming of running, where would he go?

The lizard just giggles, basking in glee,
While the hamster plots, trying to be free.
A dance party starts, with a bump and a hop,
Even the fish join in, flipping on top!

But wait, what's that? A cactus takes charge,
Waving its arms, it's feeling quite large.
With prickly fingers, it shows off its moves,
A spiky twirl that nobody grooves!

At dusk, they all settle, sharing their tales,
Of runaway socks and slippery snails.
In this wild world, laughter doesn't cease,
Together they find their own kind of peace.

Musings of the Mossy Realm

On a rock, there lies a wise old toad,
With stories of journeys thatll lighten your load.
He speaks of the great, a beetle so grand,
Who thought he could lift up the whole land.

A moss carpet dances under moon's light,
Nudging the critters to join in the fright.
A party erupts in a leafy embrace,
As worms do the worm, in a mud-splattered race.

The owls hoot out rhythm, the crickets will sing,
While mushrooms pop up, like they own the spring.
With spores in the air, they twirl and they sway,
A funky brigade, taking flight in their play.

The night wraps around them, a cozy warm quilt,
Their laughter is music, no reason to wilt.
In this earthy kingdom, where quirks intertwine,
Nature's own circus, a scene so divine!

Anthems of the Air Plants

Upon a shelf, the air plants convene,
Whispering secrets, so silly, so keen.
One claims he can fly, with a gust and a spin,
While another just giggles, saying, "Let's begin!"

They swap all their stories of raindrops and sun,
Of how they all thrive, just hanging for fun.
A clever bromeliad rolls in a pot,
Declaring its throne, in this garden plot.

A spray bottle wanders, it enters the scene,
Misting the crew, it's their good-guy routine.
Laughter erupts as they dance with the spray,
For bubbling plants, who knew life would play?

In the air, they've become quite the crew,
Making mischief under skies so blue.
For in this bright space, they grow and they laugh,
Creating their memos on joy, their own path!

Chronicles of the Closed Canopy

In the depths of green, where shadows dance,
A squirrel is plotting, a daring romance.
He's in love with a branch, but she's tough as nails,
Claiming her freedom with wind in her trails.

Each day he returns, bringing acorns galore,
She rolls her eyes, then shows him the door.
Yet, there's a charm in his hapless pursuits,
As an ant joins in, carrying odd little fruits.

The monkey swings by, a smirk on his face,
Commenting on acorns, in this funny race.
"Join us for fun, don't be such a bore,
We'll tease this poor fella till he can't take more!"

But love is a journey, through laughter and glee,
The canopy echoes with their jests, you see.
For even in nature, where chaos takes flight,
The chronicles weave joy into each night!

Lullabies of Green

In the center sits a snail,
His tiny shell, a grand detail.
He hums a tune, oh so slow,
In rhythm with the evening glow.

A bug with glasses reads a book,
Within the leaves, a cozy nook.
He turns the page, gives a sigh,
While nearby ants just march on by.

The daisies sway and start to dance,
Inviting all to join the prance.
The beetles form a jazz band there,
With fluttering wings, they strike a flair.

As night falls down, the crickets sing,
To weave a lullaby of spring.
In this green world, peace is found,
With giggles shared without a sound.

The Miniature Wilderness

A spider spins a web so fine,
He claims it's art, a real design.
A fly drops by, takes a tour,
"Is this the place where dreams allure?"

A shrew conducts a band of mice,
With tiny bows and fuzzy spice.
They play a tune that makes you smile,
Then scramble off in single file.

The lizards bask, sun on their backs,
While chipmunks plot their snacky hacks.
"Sneak in the pantry, grab a crumb!"
They giggle soft, "How'd we be dumb?"

In corners hide the secret tales,
Of mushroom kingdoms and their grails.
The grass a jungle, wild and free,
Where every creature holds a key.

Fables of Root and Leaf

A leaf declared, "I'll fly today,"
The roots replied, "You'll rue this play!"
With a gust, the leaf took flight,
And twirled around in pure delight.

A ladybug with spots so bright,
Declared a fashion show tonight.
"Red is in," she proudly said,
While ants rolled eyes, their dreams in red.

The caterpillars munch away,
On visions just for this fine day.
"Let's grow up soon, it's quite the treat!"
While moths just yawn, "We'll miss the beat."

A gnome bestowed a punny joke,
While frogs all croaked and nearly choked.
In this green place, the fun won't cease,
With tales of laughter, joy, and peace.

Reflections in the Dome

Inside the dome, the creatures rumble,
The raccoons dance, their steps a jumble.
They spin and twirl 'round tiny trees,
Chasing shadows on the leaves.

A goldfish in a tiny lake,
Wonders what the frogs might bake.
"Bake a cake? Or make a stew?"
The frogs just grin, "That'll be new!"

The wiggles of the worms below,
Make giggles soar, it's quite the show.
They twist and turn with wiggly glee,
While rabbits cheer, "Come dance with me!"

In this glass world, fun's the rule,
With laughter bright, it's quite the school.
Where every day brings new delight,
In a dome of joy, under stars so bright.

Scrolls of the Shrubs

In the garden, whispers roam,
Shrubs gossip about their dome.
A hedgehog's snore, a squirrel's dance,
Plants in bloom take a silly chance.

Ferns wear hats made of old leaves,
While daisies tell tales that the wind weaves.
A worm with glasses reads a book,
All while the gardener gives a look.

Tulips strut with great delight,
In their petals, stories ignite.
The roses chuckle, what a scene,
As the sun spills warm golden sheen.

When night arrives, the moon beams bright,
They share their dreams 'til morning light.
In this world of green and bloom,
The shrubs create their own sweet zoom.

The Story of Seeds

A tiny seed, full of dreams,
Wants to be more than what it seems.
It rolls and tumbles through the dirt,
Grumbling loudly, "Oh, this hurts!"

A bumblebee buzzes, gives a smile,
"Grow up, dear friend, it'll take a while!"
The seed looks up, gives a brave nod,
"Soon I'll sprout; I'll make them applaud!"

Poked by rain and kissed by sun,
It stretches out; it's time for fun.
A flower blooms in a dazzling show,
"Who knew I'd be such a pro?"

With colors bright, it steals the scene,
Raising laughter from the greens,
From tiny tales of a seed's quest,
Emerges joy, nature's jest!

Vows of the Vines

Two vines twist in a silly embrace,
Claiming the fence as their new space.
"I promise to climb and never fall!"
They giggle and sway, having a ball.

With each little jab, they tug and pull,
Creating a mess, their hearts so full.
"I vow to grow, and never cease,
Together, we'll spread that leafy peace!"

Around the trellis, they weave and dart,
A tapestry of laughter, a work of art.
In whispered vows, they dream aloud,
Making nature's dance a little proud.

When the wind blows, they sway with glee,
Sharing secrets with the swaying tree.
In every twist and tangled line,
Lies a love story that's quite divine.

Fables of Flora

Once in a patch where flowers bloom,
Lived a cactus with a heart like a plume.
It cracked a joke, the petals all shook,
"Life's too short, take a page from my book!"

A daffodil frowned, it didn't get fair,
"You make us giggle, but don't you care?"
The cactus replied, "Oh please, my friend,
Let's laugh together, let the fun never end!"

A dandelion puffed with laughter bright,
Told tales of winds that took flight.
"When I scatter, it's quite a spree,
Off to new homes, wilder and free!"

And so they chatted 'neath the sun's glow,
Crafting their legends in a row.
In this world of laughter, life's a song,
The flora's fables forever belong.

www.ingramcontent.com/pod-product-compliance
Lightning Source LLC
Chambersburg PA
CBHW070314120526
44590CB00017B/2679